CHINESE ART

CHINESE ART

General editor
Francesco Abbate

Translated by
Pauline L. Phillips

Octopus Books
London · New York · Sydney · Hong Kong

English version first published 1972 by
Octopus Books Limited
59 Grosvenor Street, London W1
Translation © 1972 Octopus Books Limited

Distributed in Australia by
Angus & Robertson (Publishers) Pty Ltd
102 Glover Street, Cremorne, Sydney

ISBN 7064 0027 5

Originally published in Italian by
Fratelli Fabbri Editore
© 1966 Fratelli Fabbri Editore, Milan

Printed in Italy by Fratelli Fabbri Editore

CONTENTS

PREHISTORY

China's geographical position has tended to impose on her a special kind of isolation. From the earliest times this isolation has dictated a slow evolution of traditions and customs rather than a more radical pattern of change. Chinese religious feeling, the source of all cultural forms in China, has also contributed to this slow process.

From the third millennium BC onwards, archaeological finds reveal the existence of primitive forms of agriculture in Kansu, Honan and Shantung. The different cultures in those regions, like the Yang-shao in Honan, take their names from the principal finds. Among these are many examples of plain and painted pottery, the latter decorated with simple lines of colour.

The decorations on neolithic pottery have their own magic symbolism. Their function was to propitiate the gods, that is, to make them benign. They represent man's first simple steps towards averting the threats and dangers which surrounded him in his daily life and which he attempted to remove by putting his faith in supernatural powers.

THE SHANG DYNASTY (1523–1028 BC)

It is customary to separate the history of Chinese art according to the dynasties which reigned in the land. This method will be adopted here for practical reasons, but it should not be taken too far since it is incorrect to think that with a change of dynasty there was always an immediate, automatic change in cultural and artistic fields.

The first dynasty of which we have certain knowledge is that of the Shang, who, according to most recent studies, held power from 1523–1028 BC, and whose kingdom extended over the wide plain formed by the southern curve of the Yellow River. Their last capital was at An-yang. (A mythical Hsia dynasty before the Shang is often mentioned, but there is no proper historical account of it.) It is not known for certain where the Shang people came from, although they show many affinities with the culture of Lung Shan. They appear to have practised agriculture and to have been militarily strong; they were organized socially in a hierarchy of castes at the head of which was an emperor. The art of this period is clearly imbued with a profound religious spirit and found its highest and most perfect expression in the famous ceremonial bronzes.

The divinities in whom the Shang believed were evil spirits whom they needed to propitiate with all kinds of often cruel and terrible sacrifices. For these sacrificial rituals their craftsmen created a whole series of bronze vases, many examples of which have been unearthed in the capital at An-yang. They are objects

1 *Shang period : Bronze* chili-*type vessel. Vannotti Collection, Lugano.*

1 Shang period: Bronze *chili*-type vessel. Vannotti Collection, Lugano.
Chinese bronzes, many of which were made for ritualistic use, had a range of typical shapes corresponding to their various functions. This receptacle in the *chili* group resembles the generally slimmer *ku*-type wine vessel both in the spear-head decoration at the top and in the thickening of the body. It is mounted on a ring base.

2 Shang period: *Kuang*-type wine server. Freer Gallery of Art, Washington, DC.
This example has a grooved lid terminating in the head of a fantastic animal. The decoration, which resembles that of a *t'ao-t'ieh* demon mask, is deeply incised.

3 Shang period: *Ku*-type receptacle, from An-yang. 12th century BC. Nelson Gallery of Art, Kansas City.
The sophisticated bronzes from An-yang, last capital of the Shang people, came at the end of a complex artistic evolution and demonstrate a completely mature and developed culture.

4 Shang period: Bronze *ting*-type receptacle, from An-yang. Academy of Arts, Honolulu.
The decoration of this bronze consists of a band containing three *t'ao-t'ieh* images. These correspond to the three feet of the vessel, which themselves resemble the stylized bodies of dragons. The *ting* is one of the ancient food-cooker shapes.

5 Shang period: *Yü*-type urn. Musée Cernuschi, Paris.
Apart from the crouching human figure the composition of this water container is largely made up of animal shapes.

2 *Shang period :* Kuang-*type wine container. Freer Gallery of Art, Washington, DC.*

12

4   *Shang period : Bronze* ting-*type receptacle, from An-yang. Academy of Arts, Honolulu.*

3   *Shang period : Ku-type receptacle, from An-yang. 12th century BC. Nelson Gallery of Art, Kansas City.*

13

14

of great technical quality and aesthetic merit. Although created for a practical purpose, being destined for use in sacred ceremonies, they also represent an astonishing artistic triumph. They were produced by skilled craftsmen by the *cire perdue* or 'lost wax' method. In this process the shape is first modelled in wax (usually a replica of the sculptor's original work in clay) and then covered with an outer layer of clay. The wax is next melted out in the firing while the clay retains its shape and the molten bronze is then cast in it. After cooling, the clay is cracked and the bronze image emerges.

The shape, size and decoration of these vases varied greatly according to the use to which they were to be put. There were receptacles for preparing and containing food, wine goblets and servers, water containers and vessels for ceremonial ablutions. Students in the Sung period (960–1279) identified the various types and gave each a name, often based on the dedicatory inscription incised on the inside of the vase. Among these are the *ku*, usually a wine goblet and shaped like a slender glass widening at the top, the *chüeh*, a small bowl on three feet with a beak-like handle, and the *yu*, a covered water container shaped like a bucket with a handle. The decoration always had a precise symbolic significance related to religious beliefs. Often there were representations of animals such as the dragon (*kuei*) or of demon or ogre masks (*t'ao-t'ieh*), while another recurring motif was the spiral called the *lei-wen* or 'thunder' decoration; this symbolized thunder and clouds bringing beneficial rain. Human likenesses were fairly rare in Shang art.

5 *Shang period : Yü-type urn. Musée Cernuschi, Paris.*

They did not enter the needs of the cult and had no particular significance. However, the few human faces that do appear on the bronzes are intensely expressive. The Sung bronzes show characteristics that were to become fundamental to all Chinese art; already the emphasis was placed on surface rather than on mass, on line rather than on colour. In all the decorative motifs on the bronzes there is an inner tension of line that makes them mobile and lively. Above all they express the emotional activity of their creators.

Little is known of Shang architecture since the imperial palaces, like the more modest dwellings, have completely disappeared, nor have any paintings or monumental sculptures survived as evidence. From the burial places, on the other hand, have come numerous objects of personal adornment and household religious furniture made in various materials such as bone, ivory, clay and jade.

The vases are often in white earthenware, the colour being due to the use of kaolin, a fine white clay, in their manufacture. Fragments of bone and ivory support the theory that these materials, less precious than bronze, were also commonly used. However, the most valued material and one of those most favoured by the Chinese was jade. It is splendid in both substance and colour and in spite of difficulties in working it, artists of this period succeeded in making perfect jade objects – and in doing so showed great technical skill and artistic awareness. Jade was considered the essence of purity, the symbol of life. Of the various principal shapes one, a disc of jade with a hole in the middle known as *pi*, was a symbol of the heavens and of imperial power. In addition to the ring-type *pi* there was the rectangular tube *ts'ung* that according to traditional interpretation symbolized the Earth Mother. Jade pieces featured the same animal gods as the bronzes. Jade was also used to make weapons designed for ritual sacrifice, and many daggers have a jade blade and a bronze handle sometimes bedecked with tiny turquoises. The contrast of materials and colours creates a singularly beautiful effect. So many products of the Shang period are in fact so extraordinary and so mature that it seems reasonable to see that period as the outcome of many earlier stages of civilization for which, however, evidence has still to be found.

THE REIGN OF THE CHOU (1027–256 BC)

At the end of the second millennium BC the Chou dynasty, lords of the Wei (modern Shensi), annexed the Shang kingdom and imposed its own dominion over a vast expanse of China. The Chou period is one of the most complex and stormy in Chinese history. Social and political conditions changed and important philosophical and religious movements began that were to reshape the face of China on highly individual lines. During the Chou period Lao Tzu (*c*.604–531 BC) the founder of Taoism, and Kung Tzu (*c*. 551–479 BC), better known as Confucius, were born. The philosophy of Confucius was eminently practical in its approach to problems of daily life, and, by pointing to virtue in a period of general laxity of behaviour, profoundly changed the society of the

6   *Shang period : Jade* pi-*type disc. Academy of Arts, Honolulu.*

7   *Shang period : Ritual* ts'ung *symbol in jade. Academy of Arts, Honolulu.*

8 Chou period:
Bronze figure of
an acrobat with
a bear. Freer
Gallery of Art,
Washington, DC.

9 Chou period
Wine vessel of
the yü type.
Museum of
Fine Arts,
Boston.

20

6   Shang period: Jade disc of the *pi* type. Academy of Arts, Honolulu.
According to traditional interpretation the *pi*, a pierced disc of variable size, which could be smooth or incised, symbolized the heavens and imperial power.

7   Shang period: Ritual *ts'ung* symbol in jade. Academy of Arts, Honolulu.
This ritual symbol from An-yang represents, according to tradition, the Earth Mother.

8   Chou period: Bronze figure of an acrobat with a bear. Freer Gallery of Art, Washington, DC.
In this compact and lively figurine the artist has managed to introduce a remarkable feeling of tension.

9   Chou period: Wine vessel of the *yü* type. Museum of Fine Arts, Boston.
The stylized decoration – especially the jutting animal figures on the sides – reveals how traditional shapes were modified during the Chou period, in a baroque style.

10   *Chou period:* Ts'un-*type bronze receptacle in the shape of a tiger. 10th century BC. Freer Gallery of Art, Washington, DC.*

10   Chou period: *Ts'un*-type bronze receptacle in the shape of a tiger. 10th century BC. Freer Gallery of Art, Washington, DC.
The tiger, a symbol of strength, is a popular motif in Chinese art.

11   Chou period: *Hu*-type vessel made of inlaid bronze. Vannotti Collection, Lugano.
The decoration consists of five horizontal bands in which dragons and birds pursue each other in a continuous flow.

12   Chou period: Fish and stag in jade. Metropolitan Museum of Art, New York; Rogers Fund, 1924.
Carved plaques in animal shapes are numerous, and were sewn to the clothing or fixed to the belt.

13   Chou period: Brown glaze pottery vase (top). Academy of Arts, Honolulu. Round lacquered wood box (bottom). Nelson Gallery of Art, Kansas City.
The vase has a simple incised decoration and is covered with a brown glaze. The elegant box is lacquered.

11   *Chou period :* Hu-*type vessel made of inlaid bronze.*
Vannotti Collection, Lugano.

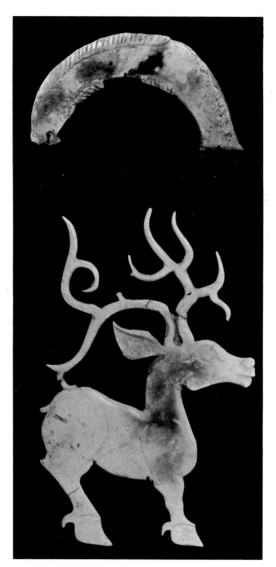

12   *Chou period : Fish and stag in jade.*
Metropolitan Museum of Art, New York.

time. Opposed to it was the religio-philosophical concept of Taoism that venerated the vital principles of nature and subsequently degenerated into magical and superstitious practices. However, it inspired many great thinkers and artists and gave important guidance to later Chinese painting. As the spirit and customs of the age became altered, so its art underwent an inevitable period of change – affecting its substance rather more than particular forms.

The populace had become more civilized and had to a great extent lost its irrational fear of demons. Often the bronzes no longer had a ritual function but adorned the homes of emperors or nobles. However, while the principal forms remained the same as in the Shang period, the style of decoration changed in spirit. Gone was the old tension of line that had represented spiritual achievement. Instead, the more elaborate modes of decoration became ends in themselves. Magical functions were overtaken by aesthetic issues, and consideration of these led to greater complexity in the planning and execution of works.

The materials used were the same as for the Shang period: bronze, jade, bone, ivory and clay. In this last field, an interesting innovation was found among tomb furnishings unearthed in the Hui-Hsien district: a series of moulded clay statuettes, full of vitality and movement, representing human figures. Their symbolic role was – it is known – to accompany the deceased into the next world; in this they took the place of the human victims that were formerly used.

In late Chou times, during a period known as that of the Warring States (480–221 BC) Chou domination gave way to a kind of political and military anarchy, and the dynastic style evolved into something more imaginative and complex. Bronze decoration was dominated by birds with curved wings, while the sinuous shapes of dragons wound themselves around vases, on the buckles and handles of swords, on the backs of mirrors, and on jewellery. The wealth of movement in this style reveals amongst other things contact with the cultures of the Asiatic steppes – the Huns and Tartars. This contact took place via the nomadic peoples who lived in the Ordos region.

The last of the Chou kings were in fact monarchs in name only. They had no effective power over the feudal nobles who then set about dividing the kingdom amongst themselves. These same feudal lords finally fought each other to extend their own domains. One of them, Lord of the Ch'in district, went from victory to victory and by 221 BC became the overlord of all China. The Chou were totally routed and he became emperor, taking the name Ch'in Shih Huang-ti (meaning First August Emperor Ch'in). His reign was violent and cruel and the Ch'in dynasty died with its founder in 206 BC, his son being soon overwhelmed by internal revolutions.

But China was united once more and remained so under succeeding dynasties. The art of the brief Ch'in period had no characteristics of its own. Fine, imaginatively decorated bronzes, terracotta statuettes and lacquered wood objects were produced in very much the same style as before. The most important innovation was the building of the Great Wall: this was started by Huang-ti and was to be continued,

13 *Chou period: Brown glaze pottery vase (top).*
Academy of Arts, Honolulu. Round lacquered wood box
(bottom). Nelson Gallery of Art, Kansas City.

14 *Chou period : Clay vase
in the shape of an owl.*
Musée Cernuschi, Paris.

15 *Chou period. Red pottery vase covered with
vitreous paste. Nelson Gallery of Art, Kansas City.*

14   Chou period: Clay vase in the shape of an owl. Musée Cernuschi, Paris.
This clay vase is similar in shape to a type of Shang bronze known as the *ts'un*.

15   Chou period: Red pottery vase covered with vitreous paste. Nelson Gallery of Art, Kansas City.
The geometric decoration is arranged in a floral pattern. The application of vitreous paste marks a new phase in Chinese ceramic art.

16   Chou period: Wooden figures. Metropolitan Museum of Art, New York; gift of M. Konor, 1948.
These stiff, angular carvings were originally enlivened by colour, small patches of which have survived.

17   Han period: Bronze censer of the *po-shan hsiang-lu* type, inlaid with gold, silver and turquoises. Freer Gallery of Art, Washington, DC.
The shape of the *po-shan hsiang-lu* is of ritual significance. The lid represents the mountain on the Isles of the Blest.

18   Chou period: Detail of a clay tomb tile. 5th-3rd century BC. Nelson Gallery of Art, Kansas City.
The offertory chambers in front of the tombs were lined with tiles in carved stone or clay; designs were impressed on the latter and then painted.

19   Han period: Bronze vase inlaid with gold and silver. Musée Guimet, Paris.
One of the main characteristics of Han bronzes is the deliberate toning-down of the ornamental motifs.

20   Han period: Bronze support in the shape of a bear. British Museum, London.
This simple but attractive figure cleverly suggests passivity and aggression in one image.

16   *Chou period: Wooden figures. Metropolitan Museum of Art, New York.*

17 *Han period : Bronze censer of the* po-shan hsiang-lu *type, inlaid with gold, silver and turquoises. Freer Gallery of Art, Washington, DC.*

18   *Chou period : Detail of a clay tomb tile. 5th–3rd century BC. Nelson Gallery of Art, Kansas City.*

19 *Han period : Bronze vase inlaid with gold and silver. Musée Guimet, Paris.*

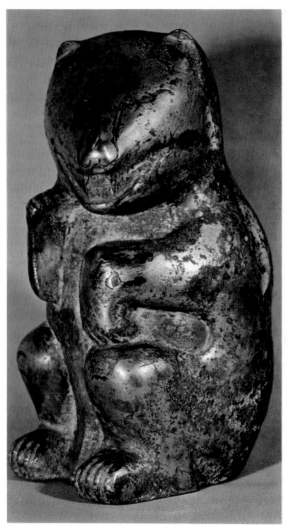

20   *Han period : Bronze support in the shape of a bear.*
British Museum, London.

fortified and completed in later periods. From then on it served as an enduring symbol of the isolation into which China continually sought to withdraw.

THE HAN DYNASTY (206 BC–AD 220)

A soldier of fortune, Liu Pang, became emperor under the name of Kao-tsu and founded the Han dynasty. For four centuries this dynasty happily ruled China, maintaining order and general well-being. Himself inspired by the wise principles of Confucius, Kao-tsu ruled intelligently and with good sense. He distributed lands to feudal lords in order to avoid trouble but he also managed to deprive those lords of regal power. He encouraged agriculture and traded with western lands via the 'Silk Route' that linked the Far East with the West.

Inevitably, in taking over such an astonishing heritage from the Shang and Chou eras, Han artists were far from indifferent to the great possibilities offered by bronze work. They were technically skilled and became increasingly expert, producing bronze basins, dishes, mirrors decorated with reliefs and opulent buckles inset with precious metals. In time the Han bronzes developed from an early style similar to that of the Chou period into one of greater sophistication. Gradually vase decoration was reduced to a minium, consisting eventually of an ornamental strip around the neck and another where the handle joined. In content these strips followed tradition and represented the *t'ao-t'ieh* or demon mask. It is significant also that these masks had by then completely lost all magical or symbolic value and had become transformed into a type of elegant ornament. On the backs of mirrors, too, the shapes of dragons and other animals formerly common in the Warring States period became progressively stylized and were later replaced by geometric decorations; these often took the form of stars, arranged around a central knob. Bronze came to be used in a variety of ways, for personal adornment and in a large number of practical and domestic objects – weapons, musical instruments, tools, etc. Specimens have also been excavated of animal figures, particularly of small bears, that may originally have served as furniture bases or supports; they are sketchily made with only a few lines but are extraordinarily expressive. The skill of the Han artists in this kind of minor art is truly notable. The animals' faces, their lively eyes and engaging poses reveal a blending of keen observation and gentle humour.

It was under the Han dynasty that the custom of glazing pottery became fairly common. A yellowish-grey glaze applied to a reddish surface, for example, resulted after firing in a pale shade of green. The production of unglazed pottery continued to survive, however. In terms of shape and decoration terra-cotta was treated in the same manner as the small bronzes. The statuettes of animals or people, usually of an everyday character, continued the tradition of the *hui-hsien* or small funerary statues of the Chou period. And in fact their purpose was the same, namely to form part of the funerary furnishings of the dead. The Chinese, like all ancient peoples, attached great importance to the after-life and when a man died they recreated in the tomb the ambience in which he had lived, surrounding the body with numerous objects that he might find useful. Few things are as evocative of the way people lived in ancient China as these finds of tiny terracotta models of houses, hay barns, carts, servants and domestic animals. It is, further-more, to these specimens that we owe our knowledge of early Chinese society and its architecture; no trace, otherwise, has survived.

The Han tombs are also interesting for their moulded stone tiles and fragments of painting. The richest regions for such finds are Honan and Shantung. In Shantung, one of the most famous tombs is that of Wu-liang-tz'u. The stone reliefs show parallel bands of horses and horsemen, Taoist sages, banqueting scenes and courtiers – a varied panorama rendered with a certain amount of perspective. The design is linear, very simple but effective. It seems probable that many of these reliefs were copies by craftsmen of paintings decorating the royal palace. Very little, however, is known about painting. The most interest-ing examples, now in the Boston Museum, show that the Han artists executed their designs on whitened bricks, using a limited range of colours.

The Han era also produced some high reliefs in stone that prefigure the monumental style of sculpture to come. Usually, as in the Shen pillars, the reliefs por-tray symbols relating to various forms of superstition. They are no longer obsessive monsters but sophisti-cated figures springing from the exquisitely poetic vein always present in the Chinese spirit: the Red Bird, symbolizing the south and summer; the Blue

22   *Han period : Painted ceramic dish.*
Nelson Gallery of Art, Kansas City.

38

21 *Han
period:
Painted
pottery
vessel.
Nelson
Gallery of
Art, Kansas
City.*

23   *Han period : Pottery figure of a dancer. National Museum, Tokyo.*   (40)

24   *Han period : Figure of a musician in polychrome terracotta. National Museum, Tokyo.*

21   Han period: Painted pottery vessel. Nelson Gallery of Art, Kansas City.
This vessel is painted with imagination and originality; the artist has made use of only two colours, black for the arabesques and bright red for the animal.

22   Han period: Painted ceramic dish. Nelson Gallery of Art, Kansas City.
Four figures in official or ceremonial dress kneel to make offerings. The work probably portrays some ritual occasion.

23   Han period: Pottery figure of a dancer. National Museum, Tokyo.
The figure is cleverly simplified and its flowing lines give it great animation.

24   Han period: Figure of a musician in polychrome terracotta. National Museum, Tokyo.
Burial objects, known as *ming ch'i,* were intended to preserve around the departed the former atmosphere of his life.

25   Han period: Model of a house in painted pottery. Nelson Gallery of Art, Kansas City.
The funerary models in terracotta offer us a faithful picture of a whole series of buildings, from the rustic barn of a country farm to a typical town house.

26   Han period: Tomb tile. Museo Nazionale d'Arte Orientale, Rome.
This incised clay tile has a popular kind of appeal. The sketchy design is partly filled with a whitish substance to stress the vitality of the figures (and also to make them easier to see).

25 *Han period : Model of a house in painted pottery. Nelson Gallery of Art, Kansas City.*

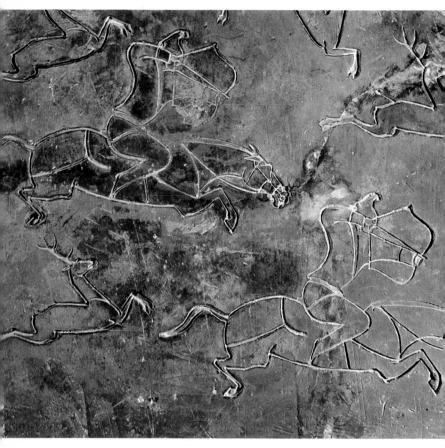

26   *Han period : Tomb tile. Museo Nazionale d' Arte Orientale, Rome.*

Dragon, symbolizing the east and spring, and the White Tiger, symbolizing the west. Artists of the Han period tended to be aware of the artistic works of the nomadic peoples of the Ordos region, an area mainly of desert situated in southern Mongolia and bounded to the south by the Great Wall. The Ordos people are still in many respects a mystery. We know only that they provided a link between the northern Asiatic steppe cultures and China. What remains of their work – mostly bronzes – reveals their enthusiasm for likenesses of animals and their skill in creating geometric decorations; the latter were often imitated by Chinese artists.

THE SIX DYNASTIES (220–590)

An uprising, due perhaps to the social inequalities that had become acute in the last years, finally put an end to the Han dynasty. The period that followed was stormy and chaotic and there were many changes of dynasty. The most important was the Tartar Wei dynasty. Of the art of this period, known generally as the Six Dynasties era, one part is in fact called Wei art; this was further divided into northern Wei (the oldest) and eastern and western Wei.

Buddhism spread into China during the Wei period through communities emigrating from India and through the preaching of wandering Buddhist monks. With the fall of the Han dynasty Confucianism, at that time regarded as the state religion, had also declined rapidly; as a result China, troubled by severe internal disorders, unsure of both her present and future, needed a new religion in which to put faith. That, broadly, is how Buddhism, which had already entered China some centuries before without making a significant mark, came to spread enormously during the Wei period. Buddhism, which is in some respects close to Christianity, answered the needs of the masses and made a new and decisive impact on art. The highest artistic achievement of the Six Dynasties was Buddhist sculpture representing the Buddha and Bodhisattvas (beings who have attained enlightenment and who remain on earth to help others). These religious images decorate caves used by Buddhist monks at, for example, Yüng-kang in the fifth century and Lung-men (sixth century). The figures were inspired by new heights of spirituality and were certainly influenced by contemporary Indian sculpture; not unexpectedly they reveal characters not found in earlier Chinese art.

The multiplicity of influences in this period brought diffusion and Wei art, unlike that of previous dynasties, has no common thread. In the caves there are decorative elements typical of central Asia, acanthus leaves and vines and sketches of capitals that are decidedly Hellenistic, together with Indian motifs of the period. The figures of the Buddha are very often dated and it is interesting to trace their evolution from a compact figure wrapped in a regularly pleated robe to a more developed type, more slender and elongated, executed with sharp lines in an angular style. In the sixth century this style softened and the lines became more fluid and sinuous; this can be seen in Lung-men sculpture. The drapery of the habit

27   *Han period : Painting on clay, from a tomb near Lo-yang. 3rd century AD.*
Museum of Fine Arts, Boston.

47

27   Han period: Painting on clay, from a tomb near Lo-yang. 3rd century AD. Museum of Fine Arts, Boston. The lively figures are outlined in ink and stand out well against their neutral background.

28   Ordos art: Bronze figure of a stag. Musée Cernuschi, Paris.
Often it is practically impossible to distinguish between original Ordos work and Chinese. Han China maintained continual contact with this nomadic people who lived to the north of the Great Wall.

29   Wei period: Buddha Sakyamuni in bronze with traces of gold. Second half of 5th century AD. Nelson Gallery of Art, Kansas City.
The best specimens of Wei sculpture are the Buddhist figures decorating the caves used by monks of the cult.

30   Wei period: Statue of Maitreya in gilded bronze. AD 477. Metropolitan Museum of Art, New York; Kennedy Fund, 1926.
Originating in India in the 5th century BC, Buddhism penetrated into China in the 1st century AD. There was an active Buddhist centre at Lo-yang.

31   Wei period: Buddha, from Yüng-kang. Second half of 5th century AD. Musée Guimet, Paris.
A feeling of gentleness and absorbed contemplation pervades this high relief image of the Buddha, a masterpiece of the 'rounded style' that is a feature of the Wei period.

28   Ordos art : *Bronze figure of a stag. Musée Cernuschi, Paris.*

29   *Wei period : Buddha Sakyamuni in bronze with traces of gold. Second half of 5th century AD. Nelson Gallery of Art, Kansas City.*

30   *Wei period : Statue of Maitreya in gilded bronze. AD 477. Metropolitan Museum of Art, New York.*

31   *Wei period : Buddha, from*
Yüng-kang. Second half of 5th
century AD. Musée Guimet, Paris.

became ever more elaborate, as did the halo behind the Buddha's head, which later came to be decorated with shining flames.

Contact with Barbarian cultures outside China gave renewed energy to Chinese decorative art, which during the Han period was reduced to graphic work of little drive or substance. Buddhism set the style for sacred architecture. As a style it remained the model for successive dynasties. The caves, decorated with paintings and reliefs, were places appointed to worship the Buddha. The pagodas were another contemporary development: these were Buddhist funerary monuments derived from the Indian *stupa*. Like them the pagoda was seen as a symbol of the world, the central pillar representing the link between heaven and earth. In the Six Dynasties period pottery also flourished. Historically it is an interesting period since it is thought to have been the time when proto-porcelain came into being: this is a type of pottery halfway between Han glazed pottery and true porcelain. It is made of a hard grey sandstone of Kaolin type and has an olive green glaze. Unfortunately, few examples survive. The *genre* was perfected by the craftsmen of a later dynasty, the T'ang.

THE BRIEF REIGN OF THE SUI (581–618)

A palace official, Yang Chien, who served at the court of Pei Chou (the last of the Six Dynasties) overthrew the emperor in 581 and took his place. So began the brief reign of the Sui (581–618), to whom nevertheless is owed the reunification of China. In 589 Yang Chien occupied the southern provinces and his son and successor, Yang Ti, built a splendid capital at Lo-yang for the new Chinese empire.

The art of the Sui period has not left any great masterpieces. It was rather a time of transition between the Wei and T'ang periods. The best Sui art consists of Buddhist-inspired sculpture. Some of the Lung-men and T'ien-lung Shan caves date from the Sui period, as do many of the rock carvings of To-shan, Yü-han Shan and other places. What distinguishes Sui Buddhist sculpture from that of the late Six Dynasties period is its fundamentally rigid structure. The figures of Buddha and Bodhisattva are severe, immobile, enfolded in drapery that has none of the the Graeco-Indian-inspired softness encountered in Wei sculpture. Some of these figures are, however, distinguished by reason of their balanced composition. We see in them a combination of the regal and the serene, a grave majesty comparable to that of the Roman consuls. There was also at this time a steady interchange of ideas between China and her neighbours, and in the west Sui sculptures were notably more sensuous and sumptuous in the Indian manner.

THE T'ANG DYNASTY (618–906)

Extravagance and social injustices in Yang Ti's reign led to the rapid fall of the Sui. They were replaced by the more fortunate T'ang dynasty. So there began, at first under the adventurer Li Yüan, the happiest and most prosperous period in China's history. China extended her domain by force of arms

32   *Wei period:* Gift bearers in procession *(detail).*
Metropolitan Museum of Art, New York.

32   Wei period: *Gift bearers in procession* (detail). Metropolitan Museum of Art, New York; Fletcher Fund, 1935.
This relief on black marble decorated a wall of the cave of Pin-yang at Lung-mên, site of a Buddhist shrine.

33   Wei period: Ceramic horse. *c.*AD 530. Academy of Arts, Honolulu.
This horse forms part of a series of funerary models and is an outstandingly naturalistic work for the period.

34   Wei period: Limestone Bodhisattva. *c.* 4th century AD. Academy of Arts, Honolulu.
The slender, tapering figure is an elegant example of the 'angular' style, which with the 'rounded' style dominated Chinese Buddhist sculpture in the Wei period.

35   Six Dynasties period: Votive stele with figure of Buddha Sakyamuni. 6th century AD. Freer Gallery of Art, Washington, DC.
Statues of the Buddha often portray him in the monk's habit that he adopted after his revelation: from this derives one of his names, Sakyamuni, the monk of the Sakya family.

36   Six Dynasties period: *Apsara* playing a musical instrument, fragment of a relief from the caves of T'ien-lung Shan. *c.* AD 570. Academy of Arts, Honolulu.
The winged figures of *apsaras* (a kind of angel of Indian mythology) often appear in Chinese Buddhist art alongside variations on the Buddhist and Bodhisattvas themes.

33   *Wei period : Ceramic horse. c 530 AD. Academy of Arts, Honolulu.*

34 *Wei period : Limestone Bodhisattva. c 4th century AD.*
Academy of Arts, Honolulu.

35 *Six Dynasties period : Votive stele with figure of
Buddha Sakyamuni. 6th century AD. Freer Gallery of
Art, Washington, DC.*

36 *Six Dynasties period :* Apsara *playing a musical instrument, fragment of a relief from the caves of T'ien-lung Shan. c 570 AD. Academy of Arts, Honolulu.*

into central Asia and to the east and south, absorbing all the small border states and pushing outward as far as India and the Caspian Sea. All kinds of trade developed and riches flowed into the nation in a continuous stream. Central Asian and western cultures, together with that of India, all made their contribution to the Chinese world. In the capital at Ch'ang-an Taoism, Confucianism, Buddhism, Manichaeism, Nestorian Christianity and Mohammedanism flourished together. China never had been, and was never again to be so cosmopolitan, yet she lost none of her own cultural unity.

The unique quality of T'ang art derives from its incomparable vigour, effective realism and nobility of form. A scholar has written that the T'ang epoch was to the Sui period what Rome was to Greece. This can be seen in the impression of assurance, dignity and security given by both the art and the civilization of the T'ang. Again, it is Buddhist sculpture that catches the attention; there were by then numerous sects spread about China, for the Buddhist religion had indeed become predominant. The influence of India and Greece are once more reflected in these sculptures – although the faces are always Chinese, as is the mobility of the drapery. As well as the sacred sculpture – the finest example being the 45-foot Buddha Vairocana at Fun-sien-ssü – there was a body of secular, imperial sculpture. Typical examples are the *lokapala* or tomb guardians (like the one from Tun-huang in the Musée Guimet in Paris). The proud bearing and physical presence of these figures faithfully reflected the prevailing image of the brave

T'ang warrior. China at that time believed in military might and entrusted herself completely to this new faith. Bronze, wood, precious metals, clay and porcelain were the materials mainly used in the very rich output of T'ang 'minor arts'. Bronze mirrors were covered with gold and silver, their backs decorated with animal figures of a truly amazing dynamism, naturalism, vitality and variety. Furniture was first lacquered and then ornamented with incrustations of mother-of-pearl, tortoiseshell, deerhorn and sometimes ivory. Musical instruments were similarly treated and richly inlaid – to great effect – with gold and silver. Ceramic ware was covered with a thick shiny layer of coloured glaze and, between the end of the seventh and the beginning of the eighth centuries, pure white translucent porcelain was made for the first time. Other splendid works of this golden age include a large quantity of elegant terracotta statuettes, which carried on the traditions of funerary art, usually representing ladies, horses, or equestrian groups. The female figures are graceful and elegant and have round faces surmounted by complicated coiffures. The horses bear witness to the love shown for them by the T'ang emperors. Prominent among the equestrian groups are the polo players, rather aloof young lords riding with elegance and composure. The most notable buildings of the T'ang period belong to the traditions of Buddhist architecture – wooden temples and many-storeyed pagodas usually made of bricks. Notable examples of these temples are to be found in Japan, where presumably they were constructed under the supervision of Chinese builders.

37 *Six Dynasties period : Cave shrine at Tun-huang, in Kansu.*
Photograph by the University of Kyoto.

38   *Sui period : Painted stone statue of a Bodhisattva.
Musée Cernuschi, Paris.*

39   *Sui period : Stone statue of Bodhisattva Avalokitesvara, from
Ch'ang-an. End of 6th century AD. Museum of Fine Arts, Boston.*

37 Six Dynasties period: Cave shrine at Tun-huang, in Kansu. Photograph by the University of Kyoto.
The oldest cave shrines in China are those at Tun-huang, a very important commercial centre in Kansu at the beginning of the Silk Route. The first temple consecrated there probably dates from AD 366.

38 Sui period: Painted stone statue of a Bodhisattva. Musée Cernuschi, Paris.
A feeling of rigid austerity often characterizes Sui Buddhist statues. The body tends to assume the form of a massive block and the face, square-chinned, is supported on a stiff, almost tubular neck.

39 Sui period: Stone statue of Bodhisattva Avalokitesvara, from Ch'ang-an. End of 6th century AD. Museum of Fine Arts, Boston.
The affinity with Indian sculpture is clear: the body curves luxuriously, the hips jut forward. The face, hands and feet are shaped with a sensuality uncommon in Chinese art.

40 T'ang period: Mirror-back in bronze laminated with silver (top); Mirror-back in bronze laminated with gold (bottom). Freer Gallery of Art, Washington, DC.
Circular bronze mirrors were greatly favoured by the Chinese, who used them for assorted toilet and magical purposes. The oldest dated specimens go back to 6 BC.

41 T'ang period: Ivory statuette of Kuan Yin. Metropolitan Museum of Art, New York; gift of A. W. Bahr, 1958.
Although the Chinese did not attribute to ivory the magical qualities associated with jade, they were very fond of it and used it to make statuettes and small-scale objects.

40   *T'ang period : Mirror back in bronze laminated with silver (top) ;
Mirror back in bronze laminated with gold (bottom). Freer Gallery of Art,
Washington, DC.*

41   *T'ang period: Ivory statuette of Kuan Yin.*
Metropolitan Museum of Art, New York.

Although the first examples of Chinese painting date from the Han period, it did not become properly established until T'ang times, when the names of painters were first recorded. It was the period of Wang Wei, the first in the tradition of literary painters. The caves at Tun-huang, a western border town, have many examples of Buddhist painting that combine Indian and Persian influences absorbed through the central Asian regions. Also from Tun-huang come many examples of weaving and paintings on silk. While for the most part the Buddhist cave paintings were carried out by fairly modest craftsmen, there were a number of artists of greater stature in existence, who lived at court under the emperor's protection. Their names have survived but very little of their work remains. Portraits of people at court were painted by Yen Li-pen, whose work shows great psychological insight into the characters of his subjects. The two greatest artists of the period, Wu Tao-tzu and Wang Wei, lived in the eighth century. The former started the 'northern' school characterized by its exuberant use of colour; the latter founded the 'southern' school, whose tendency was towards monochrome landscapes. Unfortunately, most of the work of these masters is known to us only through later copies.

THE FIVE DYNASTIES (907–60)

The end of the T'ang dynasty was not as calm as the beginning. In 845 the Buddhist shrines were ravaged by insurgents; then the Arab invasion from Asia and the advance of the Mongols stripped China of her provinces and greatly reduced her power and resources. This process of erosion led to the fall of the T'ang empire. It was followed by a period of general uncertainty and China split into several states. This period is usually known as the Five Dynasties. The art of those fifty years is of interest partly for a number of sculptures, but chiefly for some of the paintings that were produced. In the various Chinese courts painting evolved rapidly: under the Five Dynasties the greatest progress was made in the field of monochrome watercolour landscapes. The main interpreters of this type of exclusively landscape painting, called in Chinese *shan-shuei* (mountains and water), were Ching Hao, Kuan T'ung and Li Ch'eng, whose psychological approach to landscape presaged the fundamental characteristics of the Sung artists.

One of the best paintings of the Five Dynasties is the great scroll called *Deer beneath the red maples of autumn* (see illustration 51). The group of animal figures is surrounded by an autumn forest depicted with a subtle spirituality that in the changing colours of the trees catches the melancholy of the time of year. Other painters portrayed flowers, birds, and comely female figures. There was a wealth of ceramics, too, one of the major centres of development being in the north at K'ai-feng.

THE SUNG NATIONALISTS (960–1279)

The Sung, who came to power in 960, determined to reunite China and rediscover her national character by restoring her old traditions to an honoured place.

Sung China turned in on herself in the search for the spiritual light that had guided the nation in previous centuries. This was the era of the intellectual, the scholar, the philosopher, the poet and the painter, an era of culture and mysticism. Works of art were sophisticated and steeped in spirituality. The Sung succeeded in keeping China united for almost two centuries. In 1126 the Tartars occupied the northern region and the Sung withdrew to the south, moving their capital from K'ai-feng to Hangchow, a splendid city rich in sumptuous dwellings.

Painting was the major art of the Sung period. During the T'ang era the ideas of the Buddhist sect called in Chinese Ch'an (Japanese Zen) had reached China but made little impression. The movement had more success under the Sung, however, particularly in intellectual circles. The new doctrines which accepted Taoist and Confucian theories, taught that the spirit of Buddha was everywhere, in the soul of man and in the trees and rocks. It taught men to seek in Nature an ideal aspect, contemplation of which would help to induce enlightenment. This concept, so suited to the philosophical spirit of the Sung, had a notable influence on painting, and landscapes became more subjective, idealistic and lyrical in their treatment.

The Chinese usually painted on scrolls of silk or paper and in albums, and sometimes on fans. In the Sung period the greenish-blue colour predominant in the time of the T'ang gave way to painting with ink or in a variety of subtly shaded single colours. Provided they were used sparingly and watered down, both ink and colour washes were found suitable for

42 *T'ang period :
Painted wood
figure of a
lokapāla, from
Tun-huang.
Musée Guimet,
Paris.*

43 *T'ang period : Gilded bronze Buddha. Metropolitan Museum of Art, New York.*

44   *T'ang period : Painted stone figure of the Buddha.
Metropolitan Museum of Art, New York.*

42   T'ang period: Painted wood figure of a *lokapāla*, from Tun-huang. Musée Guimet, Paris.

This fierce warrior is a *lokapāla*, or tomb-guardian; his aggressive posture reflects the martial spirit of the expansionist T'ang rulers.

43   T'ang period: Gilded bronze Buddha. Metropolitan Museum of Art, New York; Rogers Fund, 1943.

This Buddha image is harmoniously proportioned and has a natural elegance, notably in the treatment of the hands.

44   T'ang period: Painted stone figure of the Buddha. Metropolitan Museum of Art, New York; Rogers Fund, 1919.

In a great deal of Buddhist sculpture Indian influences can clearly be seen; the modelling is more plastic and the figures generally are more expressive.

45   T'ang period: Glazed ceramic figure of a *lokapāla*. Victoria and Albert Museum, London.

The threatening pose, violent gesture and military costume are characteristic of some *lokapāla*, made in the belief that the more terrible they looked, the more effective they would be as protectors.

46   T'ang period: Ceramic lion biting its leg. Freer Gallery of Art, Washington, DC.

The taste for bizarre objects sometimes led T'ang artists to border upon extravagance with creations like this mottled lion in three-colour glazed ceramic ware.

47   T'ang period: Figure of a woman in ceramic ware with three-colour glaze. Victoria and Albert Museum, London.

T'ang female figurines are particularly pleasing, and here the subject reflects something of the sophisticated style of the day.

45   *Glazed ceramic figure of a* lokapāla. *Victoria and Albert Museum, London.*

46 *T'ang period : Ceramic lion biting its leg. Freer
Gallery of Art, Washington, DC.*

giving a landscape the desired sentimental, idealistic effect. The sense of perspective was suggested through atmospheric devices; the feelings inspired by a work would change as the eye passed from the trees in the foreground to the mountains beyond; these, surrounded by clouds, seemed to suggest the idea of infinity. Mist, too, was used to express the ephemeral nature of material things as compared to the immortal brilliance of ideas. Sung painting is vibrant and impassioned and spontaneous; ideally a philosophical notion was transformed in the artist's mind into a sincere poetic inspiration. The three great Sung landscape artists, Hsü Tao-ning, Tung Yüan and Fan K'uan, lived at around the end of the tenth and the beginning of the eleventh century. Kuo Hsi, Wen T'ung (d.1079) and Mi Fu also belong to the eleventh century. The first, almost all of whose work is lost, has left one written text, a stupendous *Commentary* on landscape painting. Wen T'ung is known particularly as an elegant painter of bamboos, while Mi Fu developed his own style of impressionistic painting marked by a bold use of chiaroscuro. The landscape artist Li Lung-mien also illustrated Buddhist subjects in a dignified manner. Another notably talented artist was Hui-tsung, the last emperor of K'ai-feng, who painted flowers and birds in a fresh, naturalistic style. In the new southern capital of Hangchow, the empire soon began to prosper and towards the end of the twelfth century there was a fruitful period of delicately poetic landscapists. Three of them went under the name of the 'Ma family', the brothers Ma Kuei and Ma Yüan and the latter's son Ma Lin. All could create effects of hitherto unparalleled intensity with just a few essential strokes. Ma Yüan preferred winter subjects, bare trees and houses covered in snow, to which he added foreshortened hills wrapped in a wintry kind of sadness. Ma Lin, perhaps the greatest of the three and certainly the most lyrical, painted several remarkable works portraying the stillness of evening with a tenuous and gentle melancholy. A fine example of this is the painting entitled *Waiting for friends by the light of a lantern*. Next to the Ma family, with whom he formed the Ma-Hsia school, is the great Hsia Kuei (active 1180–1230). His painting is all patches and lines in the foreground and fades in a romantic fusion of mountains, water and sky towards the horizon. Particularly effective in dealing with vast panoramas, Hsia Kuei also painted several small compositions that abound with psychological insight.

While the court welcomed this fairly large group of artists, another school arose round the monks of the Ch'an sect; it was mainly active in and near Hangchow. Although they were often considered eccentric and rebellious by people outside their circle, the monk-artists were highly accomplished, and brought to their painting a fresh spirit of nonconformism, intellectual liberty and deep religious feeling. Landscapes, portraits, flowers and animals were their subjects. Their dragons are animated with a force and vitality that seem to penetrate to the roots of existence (for the Chinese the dragon symbolized divine power and the striving of the spirit). Their flowers have a symbolic significance: the plum blossom, for instance, symbolizes the coming of spring. Their portraits are intense, crude and realistic, vibrant and with a sharpness that makes no concession to sentiment. Finally, their landscapes, as interpreted by Mu Ch'i, who was the greatest of all Ch'an artists, represent the peak of Sung painting. According to convention, Mu Ch'i lived for many years in a monastery on the shores of Lake Si-hu not far from Hangchow and his main work was concentrated in the twenty years between 1250 and 1270. A faithful interpreter of Ch'an doctrine, he translated it into animal pictures, portraits and, with a sublimity never attained before, into landscapes. He truly succeeded in giving nature a universal soul. The single elements, like his small isolated figures, his birds and fishermen's cabins swathed in silent mist, seem to pause in suspended animation. A little before Mu Ch'i there was another great painter of the Ch'an sect, Liang K'ai. He was an excellent landscapist but his portraits are still more memorable. Sometimes ironic, sometimes intensely dramatic, they are always particularly expressive. Among them is his masterpiece, the portrait of the poet Li Po (see illustration 66).

Sculpture, lacking an equivalent mystical impulse, played a minor though not inconsiderable role in this period. In fact, at the time of the Tartars Ch'i-tan and Chin, who reigned in Peking after 936, a notable renaissance of Buddhist sculpture took place, encouraged by the great respect of the Tartars for Buddhism. Sculptural themes evolved and the Bodhisattva known as Kuan Yin, became increasingly popular; he, sometimes she, was represented standing or in the 'royal relaxation' pose with one arm resting

47 *T'ang period: Figure of a woman in ceramic ware with three-colour glaze. Victoria and Albert Museum, London.*

48   *T'ang period : Glazed ceramic horse. Cicogna Collection, Milan.*

48 T'ang period: Glazed ceramic horse. Cicogna Collection, Milan.
Ceramic horses made popular funerary models, and were covered with a warm glaze imitating the shades of the hide.

49 T'ang period: *Tribute bearers*, attributed to Yen Li-pên. National Palace and Central Museum Collections, Formosa.
Horizontal scroll, ink on silk. During the T'ang period the treatment of the human figure and the features of individuals became increasingly refined.

50 T'ang period: *Playing the lute and drinking tea*, attributed to Chou Fang. Nelson Gallery of Art, Kansas City.
Horizontal scroll, ink and colours on paper. The skilful and harmonious disposition of the figures and the gay, vivid colours are characteristic of the work of Chou Fang, to whom this painting is attributed.

51 Five Dynasties period: *Deer beneath the red maples of autumn*. National Palace and Central Museum Collections, Formosa.
Vertical scroll, ink and colours on canvas. The detail in the leaves, the gentle gradation of colours and the lack of empty space echo the opulent designs on cloth and other materials that were created in the same period.

52 Five Dynasties period: *Patriarch and tiger*. National Museum, Tokyo.
Vertical scroll, ink on paper. Probably a 13th-century copy of a 10th-century painting by the artist Shih K'o. Technically as well as in the humour of the observation this work shows a new concern for brevity and precision.

49　*T'ang period :* Tribute bearers, *attributed to Yen Li-pên. National Palace and Central Museum Collections, Formosa.*

50   *T'ang period :* Playing the lute and drinking tea,
*attributed to Chou Fang. Nelson Gallery of Art, Kansas
City.*

51   *Five Dynasties period :* Deer beneath the red maples of autumn.
National Palace and Central Museum Collections, Formosa.

52   *Five Dynasties period :* Patriarch and tiger.
National Museum, Tokyo.

on the raised right knee (see illustration 69). Such figures nearly always showed creatures of opulent shape adorned with jewels and sumptuous garments – and were thus somewhat removed from the intellectual and idealistic spirit that imbued Sung secular art. The same Buddhist renaissance among the Tartars gave rise, particularly in the Hopei region, at Lo-yang and Cheng-ting, to the construction of various pagodas, places of devotion and prayer where precious relics of the Buddha or ashes of Buddhist monks and saints might be kept.

Sung ceramics are the most beautiful ever produced in China or anywhere else in the world. The output during this period demonstrates an extraordinary blend of good taste and sobriety, a sense of elegance and harmony of shape and colour. Sung ware includes thickly-glazed ceramics and translucent porcelain, and in both these kinds new peaks of perfection were reached in the techniques and excellent materials used and in the selection of glazes. These ceramics are usually divided into types according to their colour and style of decoration. There are the fine plates called *ying-ch'ing* or 'cloudy blue', the milky *ting* type that bears an incised decoration, the *kuan* with their fine crackle glaze, the brown and black glazed *chien* ware, the semi-opaque *chün* in shades of deep blue, to which patches of crimson were occasionally added, and finally the celebrated green *celadons*. Sun ceramics were and still are unrivalled in their mastery of technique and style.

THE YÜAN MONGOLS (1260–1368)

For centuries the northern frontiers of China had been threatened by the barbarian hordes, who lived a nomadic life on the northern Asiatic steppes. During the thirteenth century, when a fierce leader called Ghengis Khan put himself at the head of the Mongols, this threat became a fearful reality. Already all the northern region of China was in the hands of Tartar dynasties and these were the first to fall to the advancing Mongols. When Ghengis Khan died in 1234, half China belonged to him; his conquest was carried on and brought to a conclusion by his son and later by his grandson Kublai Khan, who in 1279 took control of the entire region. Thus began in China the reign of a Mongol dynasty, which took the name of Yüan. The dream of all nomad tribes, to reign over a great civil empire, came true for the Mongols. Even so, China did not change substantially under Mongol rule. Her heritage of art and culture remained untouched and gradually came to influence that of the Yüan themselves. Traditional forms of expression in art retained their former values. Much of this was owed to one man, Chao Mêng-fu, a highly respected descendant of the Sung imperial dynasty who lived at the Yüan court as a minister and worked to civilize the court, acting as a go-between among the new rulers and the China they had conquered. He was chiefly admired as a calligrapher. For the Chinese, calligraphy is a true art form, and Chao Mêng-fu's calligraphic works continued to be imitated during later dynasties. He was also a painter and won fame among his contemporaries with pictures of horses, a subject especially dear to the hearts of the adventurous new rulers. Beside Chao Mêng-fu four very talented painters emerged, now recognized as the four great names of the Yüan era: Huang Kung-wang, Ni Tsan, Wang Mêng and Wu Chên. Huang Kung-wang evolved a style of painting, also followed with distinction by Ni Tsan, that was rigorous, even severe in its use of form and colour.

Ni Tsan lived a simple existence and had an extraordinary gift for detecting the poetry that lay in the humble, quiet things of everyday life and for transforming them in his art. Although inspired by the early Sung painters, these two moved away from the style of Fan Kuan and Mi Fu; unlike the latter they did not seek their inspiration in spiritual isolation but in the realities of daily life. Their compositions are terse, their line dry and rather bare. They used ink sparingly, as if it were gold. Wang Mêng was very different. In his complex and agitated landscapes he reflected the violent aspects of life. Wu Chên was nearer to the southern Sung painters, developing a richer, more varied tone. There is a solemnity and composure about his work that recalls the landscapes of the tenth and eleventh centuries. Wu Chên was one of the most admired painters of bamboo. Portraying bamboo was regarded as both an affirmation of spiritual nobility and a test of technique – the latter because it was very difficult to render the leaves of the bamboo in tones of black and grey.

In all other art forms the Yüan continued the old traditions, bringing splendour but few innovations.

53   *Five Dynasties period :* Taoist temple in the mountain *attributed to Tung Yüan. National Palace and Central Museum Collections, Formosa.*

洞天山堂

54   *Five Dynasties period :* River journey in the first snows, *attributed to Chao Kan. National Palace and Central Museum Collections, Formosa.*

55   *Sung period :* Fishing in a snowy river, *attributed to Hsü Tao-ning.*
National Palace and Central Museum Collections, Formosa.

53 Five Dynasties period: *Taoist temple in the mountains*, attributed to Tung Yüan. National Palace and Central Museum Collections, Formosa.
Vertical scroll, ink and colours on silk. In Tung Yüan's paintings the landscape takes on a new importance. He eliminated colour and relied on his brushwork to give his paintings a sense of warmth and internal unity.

54 Five Dynasties period: *River journey in the first snows*, attributed to Chao Kan. National Palace and Central Museum Collections, Formosa.
Horizontal scroll, ink and colours on silk. The painting reproduced here bears the title and name of its creator written in the hand of the emperor Chan-tsung.

55 Sung period: *Fishing in a snowy river*, attributed to Hsü Tao-ning. National Palace and Central Museum Collections, Formosa.
Vertical scroll, ink and colours on silk. This is a characteristic composition in which man and his creations seem almost crushed by the towering forces of nature.

56 Sung period: *Tribute horse*. 13th century. Metropolitan Museum of Art, New York; Rogers Fund, 1941.
Vertical scroll, ink and colours on silk. A fabulous cavalcade of tribute bearers advances across a background of dark mountains that seem to brighten as it passes, reflecting perhaps the brilliance of the costumes, the banners and the trappings of the horses.

56   *Sung period :* Tribute horse, *13th century. Metropolitan Museum of Art, New York.*

Faithful to the Buddhist religion, they erected many temples and built palaces in Peking, many of which were destroyed and rebuilt in later periods. The great halls of the imperial palace, surrounded by flowering gardens and decorated in gay colours, were described by Marco Polo, who was staggered by so much richness. In sculpture, the Sung-type Buddhist statue remained while the Kuan Yin also appears frequently. The production of porcelain also continued but gradually lost that delicacy and almost miraculous perfection of the Sung period. In any event the Mongol court preferred vessels of gold and silver to porcelain. Nevertheless it was probably at this time that the famous 'blue and white' porcelain – as it became known under the Ming dynasty – made its first appearance.

THE MING (1368–1644)

China had gradually re-educated and civilized the Yüan and this was their downfall. Having lost their old ferocious ways – which had made conquerors of them – they could neither put down the minor insurrections that began to be stirred up by secret societies nor face the last, decisive revolt led by General Hung-wu. He liberated China from the Mongols and brought to power the Ming dynasty – which retained it for nearly three centuries from 1368 to 1644. Under Hung-wu and his immediate successor the capital was established at Nanking; but Yung-lo, the greatest Ming emperor, an energetic and positive man, moved it to Peking, where he built numerous

57 *Sung period* : The Isles of the Immortals, *attributed to Wang Shên and dated 1064 or 1124. National Palace and Central Museum Collections, Formosa.*

58 *Sung period* : Lotus blossoms and water birds *(detail)*. *National Museum, Tokyo.*

隔袖野名多目録
避人出鳥不成啼

59 *Sung period :* Landscape of a mountain path in
spring, *by Ma Yüan. National Palace and Central
Museum Collections, Formosa.*

57 Sung period: *The Isles of the Immortals*, attributed to Wang Shên and dated 1064 or 1124. National Palace and Central Museum Collections, Formosa.
Vertical scroll, ink and colours on silk. The tradition of the greenish-blue landscape lasted for many dynasties in China.

58 Sung period: *Lotus blossoms and water birds* (detail). National Museum, Tokyo.
Vertical scroll with the seal of Te Ch'ien, colours on silk. Flowers and animals were a favourite theme with Sung painters.

59 Sung period: *Landscape of a mountain path in spring*, by Ma Yüan. National Palace and Central Museum Collections, Formosa.
Page from an album, ink and light colour on silk. Notice how the artist has contained the greater part of his drawing in one corner of the page.

60

60 Sung period: *The hundred wild geese*, attributed to Ma Fên. Academy of Arts, Honolulu.
Horizontal scroll, ink and colour on paper. Ma Fên was the head of a whole family of painters that became particularly famous through the work of Ma Lin and Ma Yüan.

61 Sung period: *Listening to the wind in the pines*, by Ma Lin. 1246. National Palace and Central Museum Collections, Formosa.
Vertical scroll, ink and colours on silk. The theme of the painting is the emotive relationship between man and nature.

62 Sung period: *Conversation beneath the jutting pine.* National Palace and Central Museum Collections, Formosa.
Page from an album, ink and colours on silk. The signature is illegible but the page is attributed to Hsia Kuei.

61 *Sung period :* Listening to the wind in the pines, *by Ma Lin. 1246.*
National Palace and Central Museum Collections, Formosa.

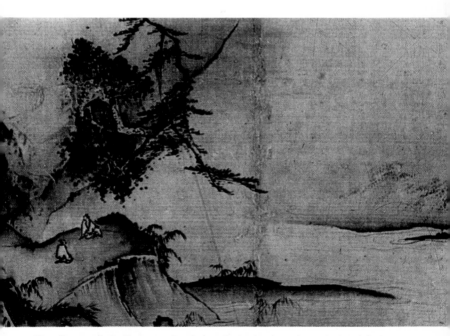

62 *Sung period :* Conversation beneath the jutting pine. *National Palace and Central Museum Collections, Formosa.*

monuments upon the ruins of Yüan buildings. The architecture of this period reveals little creativity in its structure. Its appeal lies in its richness and brilliant, gay and well-harmonized colours. To the Ming period belong some of the buildings in the sumptuous Forbidden City in Peking, the emperor's residence, some civil and religious buildings and the imperial tombs to the north of the city.

Apart from Yung-lo, the Ming emperors were almost without exception nonentities, often vicious and cruel men inclined to fall victim to palace intrigue. A climate of falsity and corruption was created around them; this in part explains why the traditional court academy – where artists protected by the emperor lived – bore little fruit. Ming painting flourished not at court but in schools and minor centres where the 'literary painters' worked. Cultured, independent students of the traditional past, they created a kind of painting in which the masterpieces were re-interpretations of ancient works. Ming painters re-made the style of the most famous Sung and Yüan landscapists, enriching it with their own originality, exceptional taste and fine technique; so much so that, judged historically, their works often reached a very high artistic level.

The most active centres of painting developed in the south in that same region where the best of the Sung artists had lived. Tai Chin, considered to be the founder of a local school known as Chê, worked at Chekiang, his native town. Wu Wei, Su Wei, Chang Lu and later Lan Ying and Ting Yün-p'êng belonged to this school. It was mainly concerned with re-

63 *Sung period :* Portrait of the master, Ch'an Wu-chün. *1238.*
Tofuku-ji, Kyoto.

64 *Sung period :* Snowy landscape, *by Liang K'ai. National Museum, Tokyo.*

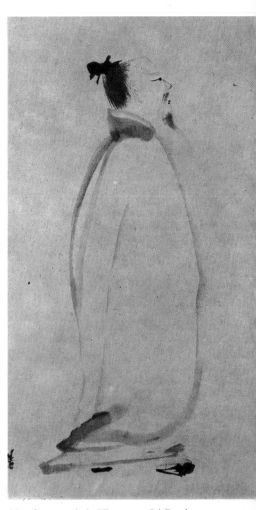

65   *Sung period :* Young
sparrows on a bamboo plant,
*attributed to Mu Ch'i. Nezu
Museum, Tokyo.*

66   *Sung period :* The poet, Li Po, *by
Liang K'ai. National Museum, Tokyo.*

63 Sung period: *Portrait of the master, Ch'an Wu-chün.* 1238. Tofuku-ji, Kyoto.
Vertical scroll, ink on silk. The artist is unknown, but the portrait is extremely attractive and well reflects the calm, benign air of the subject. The ample drapery is heightened by the use of outline colour.

64 Sung period: *Snowy landscape*, by Liang K'ai. National Museum, Tokyo.
Vertical scroll, ink and colours on silk. Painting in the Sung period found its best expression in the use of monochrome or very lightly tinted watercolours.

65 Sung period: *Young sparrows on a bamboo plant*, attributed to Mu Ch'i. Mid-13th century. Nezu Museum, Tokyo.
Vertical scroll, ink and colour on paper. This delicate work is attributed to the Buddhist monk, Mu Ch'i.

67

66 Sung period: *The poet, Li Po*, by Liang K'ai. National Museum Tokyo.
Vertical scroll, ink on paper. A few flowing lines, almost casually drawn it might seem, brilliantly evoke the whole man, the dignified figure of Li Po.

67 Sung period: *A fishing village by twilight*, attributed to Mu Ch'i. National Museum, Tokyo.
Vertical scroll, ink on paper. Through the eyes of Mu Ch'i, outlines disappear and the shapes of the landscape dissolve into a twilight uncertainty.

68 Sung period: *The screen of the nine dragons* (detail), by Ch'ên Jung. Museum of Fine Arts, Boston.
Vertical scroll, ink and light colours on paper. The flowing lines of the foreground elements contrast dramatically with the insinuating figure of the dragon.

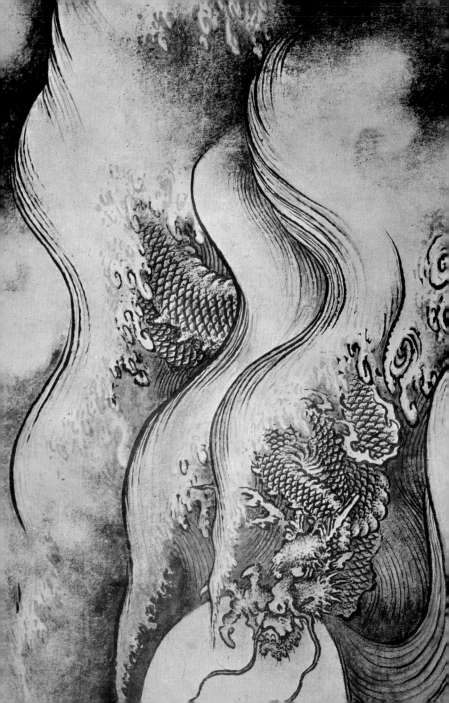

interpreting the Ma-Hsia type of landscape. The shadows and mists, however, became accentuated and some surprising touches of realism were added, particularly in the works of the master, Tai Chin. In the seventeenth century the last period of the Chê school was characterized by the elegance which informs all the compositions of Lan Ying. Another school, the Wu, took its name from Wu-hsien; in that small city were born perhaps the two greatest of the poet-painters, Shên Chou and Wên Chêng-ming. Shên Chou always lived alone, following the austere tradition of artists who impose seclusion upon themselves in order to study and work in peace. He modelled his style on the severe landscapists of the first Sung period but he also took from the manner of the best Yüan artists, particularly Ni Tsan. He also imitated Wang Mêng and Wu Chên but he was never simply an imitator. In many ways he may be considered an innovator in the landscape *genre*. There is often in his works a vibrant tension and a human warmth that makes them singularly original. When he used colour he did so with a delicacy and felicity of touch that yielded extraordinary results. Wên Chêng-ming was a poet and painter of great fame, in whose landscapes tall, craggy pines are drawn in minute detail. His style of painting was continued by his son Wên Chia and his nephew Wên Po-jên. Other artists, not in this mainstream, were Lu Chih, an exquisite interpreter of the Yüan manner and in particular of Ni Tsan; T'ang Yin, a painter of highly elaborate landscapes, who through his association with Shên Chou was often linked with the Wu

68   *Sung period :* The screen of the nine dragons *(detail), by* Ch'ên Jung. *Museum of Fine Arts, Boston.*

group, and, finally, the last great Ming painter, Tung Ch'i-ch'ang, a writer and critic, who excelled in monochrome ink landscapes.

To understand the wealth of decorative arts in the Ming period one must consider the kind of civilization that had spread with the new dynasty. Proud of having reunified China under a native dynasty, the Ming took their inspiration from the past, particularly from that period of greatest splendour, the glorious T'ang era. With the re-establishment of trade and the revival of her internal economy, China had regained her composure and began again to enjoy a taste for luxury, especially in court circles. Like the T'ang, the Ming emperors wanted to surround themselves with sumptuous textiles and furnishings and they loved pomp and elegance. This is evident in the flourishing industries making richly decorated floral patterned cloth, lacquered objects encrusted with gold and mother-of-pearl, and richly inlaid furniture. There were other, vigorous works too, such as the statues of the imperial guards, but here a certain heaviness is also apparent – especially in the abundant use of colour. The T'ang terracottas were imitated but without much success, while statuettes in ivory acquired softness and elegance.

To both connoisseurs and laymen the Ming are especially noted for their ceramics. The blue and white type, obtained from kaolin quarried near Ching-tê-chên and a type of cobalt imported from Iran, is the best known and most imitated *genre* of ceramics in the world. The dark blue decoration winds its light and sinuous way across the white

69 *Sung period : Statue of a Bodhisattva. 12th century.*
Museum of Fine Arts, Boston.

70 *Sung period : Ceramic vase of the* ts'u *type.*
Musée Guimet, Paris.

71   *Sung period :* Chun-*type vessels in blue and
violet ceramic ware. Metropolitan Museum of
Art, New York (top) and Victoria and Albert
Museum, London (bottom).*

69   Sung period: Statue of a Bodhisattva. 12th century. Museum of Fine Arts, Boston.
The soft contours of the body and its free, natural attitude are clearly of Indian Buddhist origin.

70   Sung period: Ceramic vase of the *ts'u* type. Musée Guimet, Paris.
This vase from the potteries of Tz'u Chou is decorated with a motif of peony flowers and leaves executed in black on a field of green.

71   Sung period: *Chün*-type vessels in blue and violet ceramic ware. Metropolitan Museum of Art, New York; gift of J. D. Rockefeller, jr, 1945 (top), and Victoria and Albert Museum, London (bottom).
The ceramics of Chün Chou in Honan were coloured in splendid shades of blue, violet and a reddish purple. They differed from the mainstream style of the period, which tended towards a severe monochrome, but by reason of their colour were highly prized in the West.

72   Sung period: *Ts'u*-type ceramic vessel. Metropolitan Museum of Art, New York; Rogers Fund, 1925.
At the time of the Sung dynasty, the busy potteries of Tz'u Chou were the production centre of the most important ceramic work in the whole of northern China.

72　*Sung period :* Ts'u-*type ceramic vessel. Metropolitan Museum of Art, New York.*

121

background in animal or fantasy motifs. The effect is most attractive and soon this kind of ceramic ware was being exported to many countries. Almost as famous are the three-colour and five-colour ceramics (the former usually green, yellow and violet, the latter with light blue and red as well) with beautiful floral decorations on a pure porcelain background. The other best known type of Ming ware was the monochrome vessel in ferrous red, black or dark blue. Even though Ming ceramics did not achieve the purity and inimitable elegance of Sung work, they often had the variety, splendour and dewy freshness of a flower garden. Sung art had been completely spiritual and in ceramic ware craftsmen had sought a limpid crystalline beauty, bare and severe, free from facile effects. With the Ming, the material took the upper hand again but it was a splendid material, animated and enlivened as though by a breath of spring.

THE CH'ING (1644–1912)

Another dynasty of foreign origin was destined to profit by the internal upheavals of the Chinese empire and to conquer it by force of arms, namely the Manchu leaders who occupied Peking in 1644. The result was a new emperor and a new dynasty. The new rulers were the Ch'ing, who remained firmly in power until 1912, when the republic was proclaimed. The Ch'ing, too, showed respect for the civil and cultural traditions of the conquered land. The Ch'ing dynasty owes its main fame and its most positive achievements to three emperors: K'ang-hsi (1662–

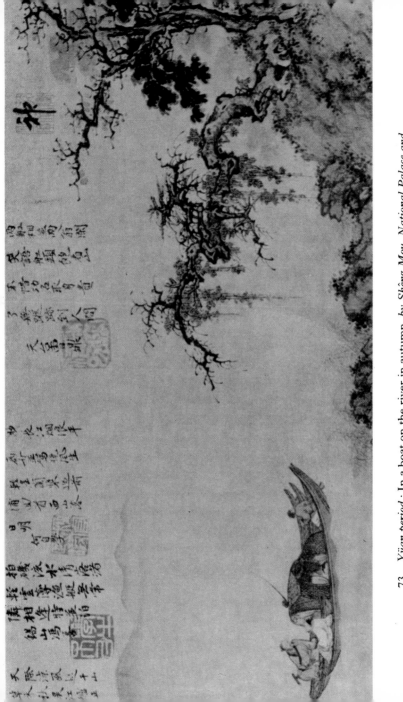

73 *Yüan period* : In a boat on the river in autumn, by *Shêng Mou. National Palace and Central Museum Collections, Formosa.*

123

74 *Yüan period :* Bamboo. *National Palace and Central Museum Collections,*
Formosa.

75   *Yüan period :* Mountain scene with a cottage by
a river, *by Ni Tsan. 1372. National Palace and
Central Museum Collections, Formosa.*

73   Yüan period: *In a boat on the river in autumn*, by Shêng Mou. National Palace and Central Museum Collections, Formosa.
Horizontal scroll, ink and colours on paper. The lively and somewhat unusual design of the scroll is a revival of the 'corner' composition characteristic of some Sung landscapes (see illustration 59).

74   Yüan period: *Bamboo*. National Palace and Central Museum Collections, Formosa.
Ink and colours on paper. This is a detail from an album of twenty pages by the painter Wu Chên, dated 1350.

75   Yüan period: *Mountain scene with a cottage by a river*, by Ni Tsan. 1372. National Palace and Central Museum Collections, Formosa.
Vertical scroll, ink on paper. The simplicity of Ni Tsan's work is particularly prized by the Chinese.

76   Yüan period: *Bamboo and chrysanthemums* by K'o Chiu-ssu. National Palace and Central Museum Collections, Formosa.
Vertical scroll, ink on paper. The bamboo theme, popular with Yüan painters, is here painted in monochrome.

77   Yüan period: *Cabins near the hills in autumn*, by Wang Mêng. National Palace and Central Museum Collections, Formosa.
Vertical scroll, ink and colours on paper. This painting by Wang Mêng is outstanding for the variety of tones, the sparing use of colour and the unity of its composition.

76   *Yüan period :* Bamboo and chrysanthemums, *by K'o Chiu-ssu. National Palace and Central Museum Collections, Formosa.*

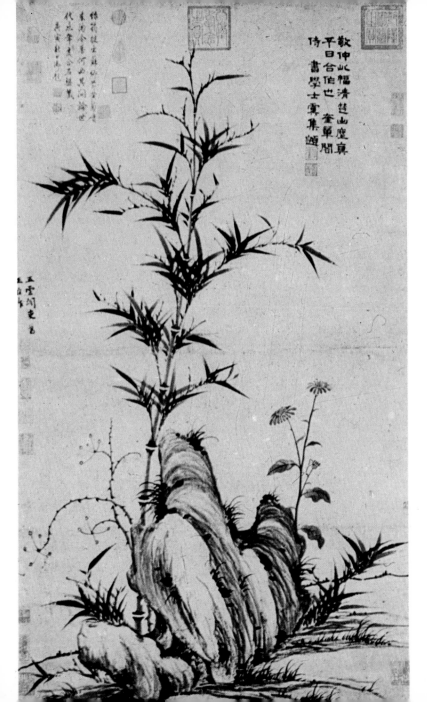

1722), Yung Chêng (1723–35), and Ch'ien Lung (1736–95). These three men were largely responsible for China's artistic renaissance in the seventeenth and eighteenth centuries. At their courts lived writers, artists and Jesuit priests from the West, who contributed certain influences to the development of Chinese architecture, painting and ceramics.

At the same time, the artistic work of this period conquered the West and spread the taste for *chinoiseries*. The three emperors named above were outstanding builders. They ordered the principal palaces and monuments erected in previous eras, such as the Summer Palace, to be restored, extended and enriched. Thanks to the planning of the Italian Jesuit, Castiglione, and later of the French priest Père Benoit, the Summer Palace was transformed into a kind of Versailles. Unfortunately the fountains and pavilions of the new complex have since been partly destroyed.

Surviving examples of Ch'ing architecture include some pavilions in the imperial residential quarters (the Forbidden City), among which are the Gateway of Supreme Harmony, the audience chambers and the splendid Altar of Heaven. This architecture faithfully followed Ming models and therefore seems comparatively poor in conception and structure, although its final effect is pleasing – in a rather fabulous way.

In a corner of the Forbidden City in Peking was a studio where Chinese artists of the Court Academy worked alongside artists from the West. This was how academic painting came closer to Western taste, as

77 *Yüan period :* Cabins near the hills in autumn, *by Wang Mêng.*
National Palace and Central Museum Collections, Formosa.

78   *Yüan period: Statue of Kuan Yin in painted and gilded wood. Nelson Gallery of Art, Kansas City.*

79   *Ming period : Figure of a guard in glazed ceramic ware. Nelson Gallery of Art, Kansas City.*

80　*Ming period :* The farewell, *by Wên Chêng-ming, 1531.*
Vannotti Collection, Lugano.

132

81 *Ming period:* Fishermen on a river in autumn, *by T'ang Yin.*
National Palace and Central Museum Collections, Formosa.

78   Yüan period: Statue of Kuan Yin in painted and gilded wood. Nelson Gallery of Art, Kansas City.
On the half-naked body of the god, scarves and necklaces are knotted and intertwined in a continuous play of sinuous lines, producing an extraordinary pictorial effect.

79   Ming period: Figure of a guard in glazed ceramic ware. Nelson Gallery of Art, Kansas City.
This magnificent figure of a guard, in glazed ceramic ware, once adorned the roof of a pagoda. Its stylized, swirling lines convey an awesome kind of controlled aggression.

80   Ming period: *The farewell*, by Wên Chêng-ming, 1531. Vannotti Collection, Lugano.
Vertical scroll, ink and colours on paper. The relationship between the men and the trees reinforces the atmosphere of separation.

81   Ming period: *Fishermen on a river in autumn*, by T'ang Yin. National Palace and Central Museum Collections, Formosa.
Horizontal scroll, ink and colours on silk. The fishermen and onlookers live quietly in the dominating presence of the rocks.

82   Ming period: *Two fishermen on a river, with plane trees*, by Shên Chou. Academy of Arts, Honolulu.
Vertical scroll, ink and colours on paper. This work, carried out in a rather stiff manner, is notable for its peculiar perspective.

83   Ch'ing period: First courtyard and building of the T'ai-ho Mên, in the Forbidden City, Peking.
Beyond the courtyard rises the T'ai-ho Mên, or Gateway of Supreme Harmony. Through this pavilion the imperial way led to the San Ta Tien, or Audience Chamber.

82 *Ming period :* Two fishermen on a river, with plane
trees, *by Shên Chou. Academy of Arts, Honolulu.*

83   *Ch'ing period : First courtyard and buildings of the*
T'ai-ho Mên, in the Forbidden City, Peking.

Chinese artists became more concerned with realism and technical effects of shading and chiaroscuro. There were, however, no painters of great quality in the Academy. There was more talent to be found among the independent literary painters and artists, who followed traditions started in the Yüan and Ming periods.

The Ch'ing literary groups learnt nothing from the West. They preferred to study the masters of the past, particularly of the Sung and Yüan periods, and this gave rise to eclectic works combining both skill and sincerity. The six great names of the Ch'ing period belong to the literary group: the Wang (Wang Shih-min, Wang Chien, Wang Hui and Wang Yüan-ch'i), Wu Li and Yün Shou-p'ing. Of the four Wang, the first two imitated with great sensitivity of line the best Yüan landscapists without quite achieving their degree of tension. Wang Hui was somewhat more talented: he was skilful at imitating the styles of various masters while still maintaining his own personality. Certain of his exuberant and complex landscapes recall Wang Mêng, but compared with the latter's irrational violence, there is an inner balance which governs all Wang Hui's compositions. Wang Yüan-ch'i was certainly the greatest of the four. Because of his originality of conception and surprising use of colour, he is closer to the Individualist painters than to the literary group. Wu Li, however, remained close to the literary tradition, concentrating on the study and interpretation of the masters; though his conversion to Catholicism did influence his painting and brought about a refined eclecticism in landscapes of exquisite workmanship. The last of the six great names, Yün Shou-p'ing, saw – and admitted – that the Wang surpassed him in landscape painting. He therefore dedicated himself to pleasant floral subjects enlivened by an extraordinary beauty of colour, which became very popular.

The group of painters which arouses the greatest interest in the Ch'ing period is undoubtedly that of the Individualists, or 'rebels' as they came to be called by analogy with the Ch'an rebels in the Sung period. They too were usually monks of the Buddhist faith living as recluses and paintings on lines radically opposed to the official style. At times their work was wild and exaggerative but generally they worked with

84   *Ch'ing period : The Imperial Summer Palace, Peking.*

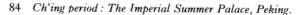

the quality, inspiration, passion and imagination of true creators. Kung-hsien wrapped his meagre and misty landscapes in an atmosphere of still and silent drama. Pa-ta-shan-jên (also called Chu Ta) turned his back on the world, rejected all the stylistic tendencies of his time and, with a few broad brush-strokes in pictures almost without design, succeeded in giving the essence of life and form to all his compositions. Shih-t'ao blended the spirit and appearance of his subjects with a consistent freshness and sense of emphasis. His painting is like a song that slowly unfolds, embracing mountain and tree, cabin and stream.

In the wake of the Ming the splendid ceramic tradition

85 *Ch'ing period : The Imperial Summer Palace, Peking.*

86   *Ming period :* Mei-p'ing-*type vase in porcelain.*
Musée Guimet, Paris.

84–85 Ch'ing period: The Imperial Summer Palace, Peking.
Outside the Forbidden City, on the hills surrounding Peking, the imperial summer residence was laid out in a succession of gardens and palaces.

86 Ming period: *Mei-p'ing*-type vase in porcelain. Musée Guimet, Paris.
The *mei-p'ing* vases were intended to hold a single sprig of plum blossom; their shape is characteristic of the Ming period.

87 Ch'ing period: *Mountain landscape*, by Wang Chien. Freer Gallery of Art, Washington, DC.
Vertical scroll, ink and colours on paper. Note the minute attention to detail and the command of perspective.

88 Ch'ing period: *River landscape* by Kung-hsien. Nelson Gallery of Art, Kansas City.
Horizontal scroll, ink on paper. This landscape seems

88

based on a direct observation of nature and shows resourcefulness in the use of ink tones.

89 Ming period: *Hu-li-hung*-type porcelain bowl. National Palace and Central Museum Collections, Formosa.
The fruits are in copper red. This type of decoration is decidedly rare because it is difficult to produce.

90 Ming period: Porcelain dish with 'five-colour' glaze. Campilli Collection, Rome.
A gay motif of leaves, flowers and birds covers this beautiful porcelain 'five-colour' dish.

91 Ch'ing period: *Landscape*, by Wang Shih-min. 1647. Vannotti Collection, Lugano.
Vertical scroll, ink on paper. This work, according to its author, was inspired by the style of Huang Kung-wang.

89   *Ming period : Hu-li-hung-type porcelain bowl.*
National Palace and Central Museum Collections,
Formosa.

90   *Ming period : Porcelain dish with 'five-colour' glaze.*
Campilli Collection, Rome.

91   *Ch'ing period :* Landscape, *by Wang Shi-min.*
1647. Vannotti Collection, Lugano.

– the pride of Chinese art – continued. The regions of the three emperors mentioned earlier, K'ang-hsi, Yung Chêng and Ch'ien Lung, spanned the most important developments in Ch'ing ceramics. The Ming types continued but were gradually changed by the addition of new colours and glazes and by ever more complex and fantastic decorative themes. In the time of K'ang-hsi the Ming five-colour ceramics developed into the range known as the *famille verte* after its dominant colour. Other groups were known as *famille noire* and *famille jaune*; later the softer, more refined *famille rose* came into favour; another variety was the *mille-fleurs* type. The ceramics belonged in a long and flourishing tradition and the emperors were enthusiastic connoisseurs and always demanded the best. The result was work of enormous richness and variety.

This was the age of true painted porcelain, decorated with delicate landscapes, birds and flowers. At the same time a range of sophisticated monochrome vases was still produced, the most remarkable being the red type known as *sang de boeuf*. After the eighteenth century, China merely retraced her steps into the past and her art fell into decadence. Only in the twentieth century was progress made, this time in painting. Towards the beginning of the century, many young Chinese painters went to Paris and absorbed the artistic climate there. When they returned home, they opened studios in Peking, Nanking and Shanghai and sought to recreate the atmosphere of Paris; there, to some extent, Western influence has continued to survive.

92 *Ch'ing period : Figure of Kuan Yin in white porcelain. Campilli Collection.
Rome.*

94 *Ch'ing period :* The coming of autumn, *by Hung Jên.*
Academy of Arts, Honolulu.

95   *Ch'ing period :* Famille verte
*porcelain vase. Metropolitan Museum
of Art, New York.*

96 *Ch'ing period :* Famille noire *porcelain vase. Nelson Gallery of Art, Kansas City.*

92   Ch'ing period : Figure of Kuan Yin in white porcelain. Campilli Collection, Rome.

The Kuan Yin statuettes were modelled with soft lines and delicate drapery and created effects similar to those of carved ivory.

93   Ch'ing period: *Landscape in the style of Tung Ch'i-ch'ang*, by Wang Yüan-ch'i. 1710. Vannotti Collection, Lugano.

Vertical scroll, ink and light colours on paper. Wang Yüan-ch'i drew his inspiration from the forms used in earlier times, reorganized to suit personal objectives.

94   Ch'ing period: *The coming of autumn*, by Hung Jên. Academy of Arts, Honolulu.

Vertical scroll, ink on paper. This Hung Jên landscape is as fragile and delicate as a castle of glass.

95   Ch'ing period: *Famille verte* porcelain vase. Metropolitan Museum of Art, New York; gift of B. Altman, 1913.

The cylindrical shape of this vase is characteristic of the period and its predominantly green colouring is also true to type.

96   Ch'ing period: *Famille noire* porcelain vase. Rockefeller Collection, Nelson Gallery of Art, Kansas City.

A motif of flowers, rocks and birds stands out sharply against a black background; the dragon-shaped handles are left white.

97   Ch'ing period: Miniature vase bearing the mark of Ch'ien Lung Nien Hsi. Metropolitain Museum of Art, New York; gift of Kate Read Blacque.

This elegantly shaped vase shows a more daring balance of colour and design than the two previous examples – though its overall harmony is unimpaired.

97　*Ch'ing period : Miniature vase bearing the mark of Ch'ien
Lung Nien Hsi. Metropolitan Museum of Art, New York.*

BIBLIOGRAPHY

M. BATTERBERRY, Chinese & Oriental Art, New York, 1969

M. BUSSAGLI, Chinese Bronzes, London & New York, 1969

H. G. CREEL, The Birth of China, London, 1936 and New York, 1954

A. FRANK, Chinese Blue and White, New York, 1969

B. KARLGREN, Yin and Chou in Chinese Bronzes, BMFEÅ, VIII, 1936; IX, 1937

A. SALMONY, Archaic Chinese Jades, Chicago, 1952

L. SICKMAN & A. SOPER, The Art and Architecture of China, London, 1966

O. SIREN, History of Early Chinese Art, 4 vols, London, 1929–30 and 2 vols, New York, 1970
   The Chinese on the Art of Painting, New York, 1963
   Chinese Painting, London, 1956

P. C. SWANN, Chinese Painting, New York, 1967

W. WILLETTS, Chinese Art, 2 vols, London, 1958
   Foundations of Chinese Art, New York, 1965

INDEX OF ILLUSTRATIONS

157